Backyard Animals
Sparrows

Christine Webster

Weigl Publishers Inc.

Published by Weigl Publishers Inc.
350 5th Avenue, Suite 3304, PMB 6G
New York, NY 10118-0069
Website: www.weigl.com

Library of Congress Cataloging-in-Publication Data

Webster, Christine.
  Sparrows / Christine Webster.
      p. cm. -- (Backyard animals)
  Includes index.
  ISBN 978-1-59036-681-3 (hard cover : alk. paper) -- ISBN 978-1-59036-682-0 (soft
cover : alk. paper)
  1. Sparrows--Juvenile literature. I. Title.

QL696.P2W37 2008
598.8'83--dc22

                                                            2006102109

Printed in the United States of America
  2 3 4 5 6 7 8 9 0 11 10 09 08

Editor Heather C. Hudak
Design and Layout Terry Paulhus

Cover: People brought house sparrows to Brooklyn, New York, from Europe in the
early 1850s. Today, they can be found all over North America.

Contents

Meet the Sparrow

The word *sparrow* means "small birds." Sparrows are small, plump, seed-eating birds. Most are about 6 inches (15 centimeters) long and weigh less than 2 ounces (57 grams). Sparrows often are dull brown or gray in color. They have a stubby beak that is used for cracking seeds.

Sparrows easily **adapt** to many environments. They live in swamps, prairies, forests, marshes, and deserts. Sparrows often live near people and buildings. They tend to live together in **colonies**.

Many sparrows live in the same place year-round. However, some sparrows **migrate** south for the winter. Older male sparrows may choose to winter near their breeding, or mating, area.

A sparrow may swim if it is trapped or to escape a **predator**.

In cold weather, a song sparrow must eat between 85 and 4,000 seeds in one hour.

All about Sparrows

Sparrows are found all over the world. There are about 50 **species** of sparrows in North and South America. They include song sparrows, house sparrows, tree sparrows, and lark sparrows.

There are two main groups of sparrows. They are the Old World Sparrows and the New World Sparrows. Both groups have short, strong beaks for eating seeds.

Sparrows' feet are designed for sitting on thin branches or perches.

Colors of Sparrows

American Tree
- Has a reddish-brown cap, grayish face, and grayish-white breast

Song
- Has a streaked chest with a spot in the center

Savannah
- Has a yellowish stripe over each eye

Lark
- Has a fan-shaped black tail with white tips

White-crowned
- Has two black stripes and one white stripe on its head

Sparrow History

House sparrows are **native** to Europe and parts of Asia and Africa. European settlers brought the first sparrows to North America in the 1850s. Their trees were being destroyed by insects. The settlers wanted the house sparrow to eat the insects.

At first, this plan worked well. However, the house sparrow **population** soon grew. There were so many house sparrows that they began to eat crops and fruit trees. The sparrows also took over the nests of native birds. Today, the house sparrow is considered a pest by some people.

Fascinating Facts

There are more than 150 million house sparrows living in North America.

House sparrows are small, stocky birds.

Sparrow Shelter

Many sparrows live in cities. Some live in forests. Others live in swampy marshes, on prairies, or in deserts.

Most sparrows build nests in clumps of grass on the ground. They also build nests in shrubs and low trees. Often, the nests are near the ground. This puts sparrows at risk of attack from predators. Cats, dogs, raccoons, snakes, and owls are predators of sparrows.

A sparrow's nest is well built. It is small and cup-shaped. The nest is made of grass, plant fibers, and small twigs. Some sparrows add feathers, hair, moss, or bark to their nests.

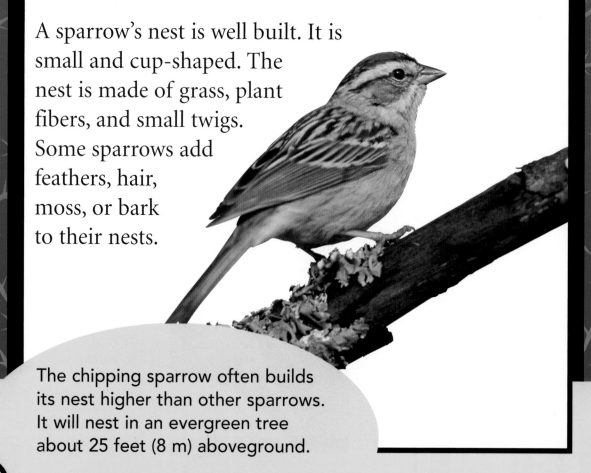

The chipping sparrow often builds its nest higher than other sparrows. It will nest in an evergreen tree about 25 feet (8 m) aboveground.

Many sparrows have their own song or pattern when they chirp.

Sparrow Features

All sparrows have similar features. Their dull coloring allows them to blend in with trees. They also hide easily in long grass. A sparrow's many features are adapted for daily life.

BEAK
Some sparrows have a longer beak in the summer. This is because they eat softer foods. In the winter, the seeds are harder and wear down the beak.

FEATHERS
Feathers keep sparrows warm and help them to fly. A sparrow's chest feathers are often speckled with color. There are colorful markings on the head, too.

TAIL

The tail of a sparrow is made of longer feathers. The tail may be short and rounded or long and rounded.

FEET

Sparrows have four toes on each foot. Three toes point forward. The largest and strongest toe faces backward. Sparrows use their toes to scratch at the ground. They dig for seeds or other foods.

What Do Sparrows Eat?

Seeds are sparrows' main food for winter. Sparrows eat all types of seeds. These include corn, wheat, sunflower, pumpkin, and grass seeds. Sparrows use their large feet to scratch for seeds. Then they crack open the tough seeds with their beaks. Sparrows also like to eat fruits and berries. They may eat crumbs left by humans.

In summer, sparrows add insects to their diet. Insects are easier to find in warmer weather. Sparrows use their feet to dig for small insects. Then they grab the insect with their beak. An adult sparrow will place the insect inside the mouths of its babies.

Fascinating Facts

A swamp sparrow has the longest legs of any sparrow species. It can wade in shallow water to search for food. Sometimes, a swamp sparrow will put its head under water to catch **prey**.

Some sparrows fly from a perch to catch flying insects, such as dragonflies.

Sparrow Life Cycle

In early spring, sparrows mate in the northern parts of North America. Soon after, the female lays four or five eggs in the nest. About 2 weeks later, the eggs hatch.

Eggs

Different types of sparrows lay different colors of eggs. The eggs may be white and speckled, pale green, or blue. Most often, the female sits on the eggs to keep them warm.

Baby

About 10 days after hatching, baby birds leave the nest. Some may hop around on the ground nearby for a few days. Others will fly away. When a baby sparrow has all of its feathers, it is called a fledgling.

A female sparrow may have four sets of babies in one year. Baby birds are dependent on their parents. Both males and females care for the baby birds. The parents collect insects to feed their young.

Adult

A house sparrow is considered to be an adult at about 15 days of age. At this age, it is about the same size as its mother. Adult sparrows often build their nests near others of their species. In nature, sparrows live between one and two years.

Encountering Sparrows

Baby sparrows often leave the nest before they can fly. If a baby sparrow is hopping around on the ground, often its parents are nearby. It is important to leave the baby bird alone. Keep pets, such as dogs and cats, away from the baby bird.

Sometimes baby sparrows fall out of the nest or are blown out by a gust of wind. If the bird is injured, it is best to call a wildlife officer for help. Keep the bird in a warm, dark place until help arrives. A small cardboard box works well.

Some people enjoy watching birds in their yard. They have birdhouses to attract sparrows. A birdbath filled with water and a bird feeder will also attract sparrows.

Useful Websites

To learn more about house sparrows, check out **www.birds.cornell.edu/AllAboutBirds/ BirdGuide/House_Sparrow.html**

Sparrows prefer to eat on the ground, but some types will eat seeds from a feeder.

Myths and Legends

Sparrows are some of the most common birds. From Japan to North America, cultures all over the world tell stories about sparrows. These birds are even mentioned in the Bible.

In one Japanese tale, a couple helps a hungry sparrow. The sparrow repays the couple by singing for them. However, an angry neighbor cuts the bird's tongue to stop him from singing. The couple searches for the hurt sparrow. When they find him, the bird offers  them one of two baskets. One basket is very large, and the other is small. The couple takes the small basket. At home, they learn it is filled with treasure. Seeing this, the neighbor visits the sparrow. He offers her one of two baskets. The woman takes the large basket, only to find it is filled with terrible creatures.

Some white-crowned sparrows do not travel far from where they are born. Others migrate in flocks.

Why Trees Lose Their Leaves

This is a Cherokee legend about a sparrow.

In early times, animals talked to trees. Each winter, birds flew south to warmer places. One year, Sparrow was injured and was not able to fly. He sent his family south without him. Sparrow knew he would not survive the cold, so he asked Oak tree if he could take shelter in his leaves. However, the crusty tree did not want to help. Next, Sparrow went to Maple. Maple did not want to help. Finally, Sparrow went to Pine. Pine was happy to share his tiny leaves with the bird.

Creator saw that the other trees had refused to help Sparrow. He called the trees together. Creator said that each winter, the trees' leaves would dry up and blow away. Creator told Pine he was pleased with him. Pine, who had the least, gave the most. For this, Pine would remain green throughout all of the seasons.

Frequently Asked Questions

How do house sparrows clean their feathers?

Answer: House sparrows clean their feathers by rolling around in soil and dust. This is called a dust bath.

Do sparrows feed milk to their babies?

Answer: Birds do not produce milk for their babies. Instead, adult sparrows dig for insects and carry them to the nest for their young.

Where do house sparrows nest?

Answer: House sparrows build messy nests in small openings in trees and buildings. They are aggressive, and sometimes, they take over the nests of other birds.

Puzzler

See how much you know about sparrows.

1. How many toes do sparrows have on each foot?
2. Where do most sparrows build their nests?
3. How many sparrows live in North America?
4. What do sparrows eat?
5. How many eggs does a female lay at one time?

Answers: 1. four 2. on the ground or low to the ground 3. about 150 million 4. seeds, crumbs, fruits, berries, and insects 5. four or five eggs

Find Out More

There are many more interesting facts to learn about sparrows and other birds. If you would like to learn more, look for these books at a library near you.

Herkert, Barbara. *Birds in Your Backyard.* Reader's Digest, 2004.

Stokes, Donal and Lillian. *Stokes Backyard Bird Book.* Rodale, 2003.

Words to Know

adapt: to adjust to the natural environment

colonies: groups that live together

migrate: move from one place to settle in another

native: an original animal to the area

population: the number of people or species in an area

predator: an animal that hunts other animals for food

prey: animals that are hunted by other animals for food

species: a group of animals or plants that have many features in common

Index